W9-BOM-956

# Cardinals

ABDO
Publishing Company

A Buddy Book
by
Julie Murray

**VISIT US AT**
**www.abdopub.com**

Published by Buddy Books, an imprint of ABDO Publishing Company, 4940 Viking Drive, Suite 622, Edina, Minnesota 55435. 

Printed in the United States.

Edited by: Christy DeVillier
Contributing Editors: Matt Ray, Michael P. Goecke
Graphic Design: Maria Hosley
Image Research: Deborah Coldiron
Cover Photograph: Digital Stock
Interior Photographs: Digital Stock, Getty Images

**Library of Congress Cataloging-in-Publication Data**

Murray, Julie, 1969-
Cardinals/Julie Murray.
p. cm. — (Animal kingdom)
Summary: Describes the physical characteristics, behavior, and habitat of cardinals.
ISBN 1-57765-704-7
1. Northern cardinal—Juvenile literature. [1. Northern cardinal. 2. Cardinals (Birds)] I. Title. II. Animal kingdom (Edina, Minn.)

QL696.P2438 M87 2002
598.8'83—dc21

2001053722

# Contents

# Cardinals

There are over 9,000 **species**, or kinds, of birds. Some bird species live near people in their backyards. Some of the best-known backyard birds are cardinals.

Cardinals, sparrows, robins, and orioles are songbirds. The cardinal song sounds like a whistle or a flute. Male and female cardinals sing the same song. It is common to see a cardinal singing near its mate.

# What They Look Like

Cardinals have feathers that stand up on their heads. This is the cardinal's **crest**. The cardinal's crest makes its head look pointed.

Male and female cardinals are the same size. These birds are seven to nine inches (18 to 23 cm) long. They weigh about one and a half ounces (43 g).

A male cardinal

A female cardinal

Male cardinals are easy to spot. The male cardinal is bright red. The female cardinal is brownish with some red on her head, wings, and tail. Both male and female cardinals have black feathers around their beaks.

# Feathers

A cardinal's feathers are very important. Feathers help to keep cardinals warm in the winter. Feathers help to keep cardinals dry when it rains, too.

There are three kinds of bird feathers. Flight feathers are the longest feathers. Body feathers are shorter and softer. Down feathers lie closest to a bird's body. Down feathers are very soft and fluffy.

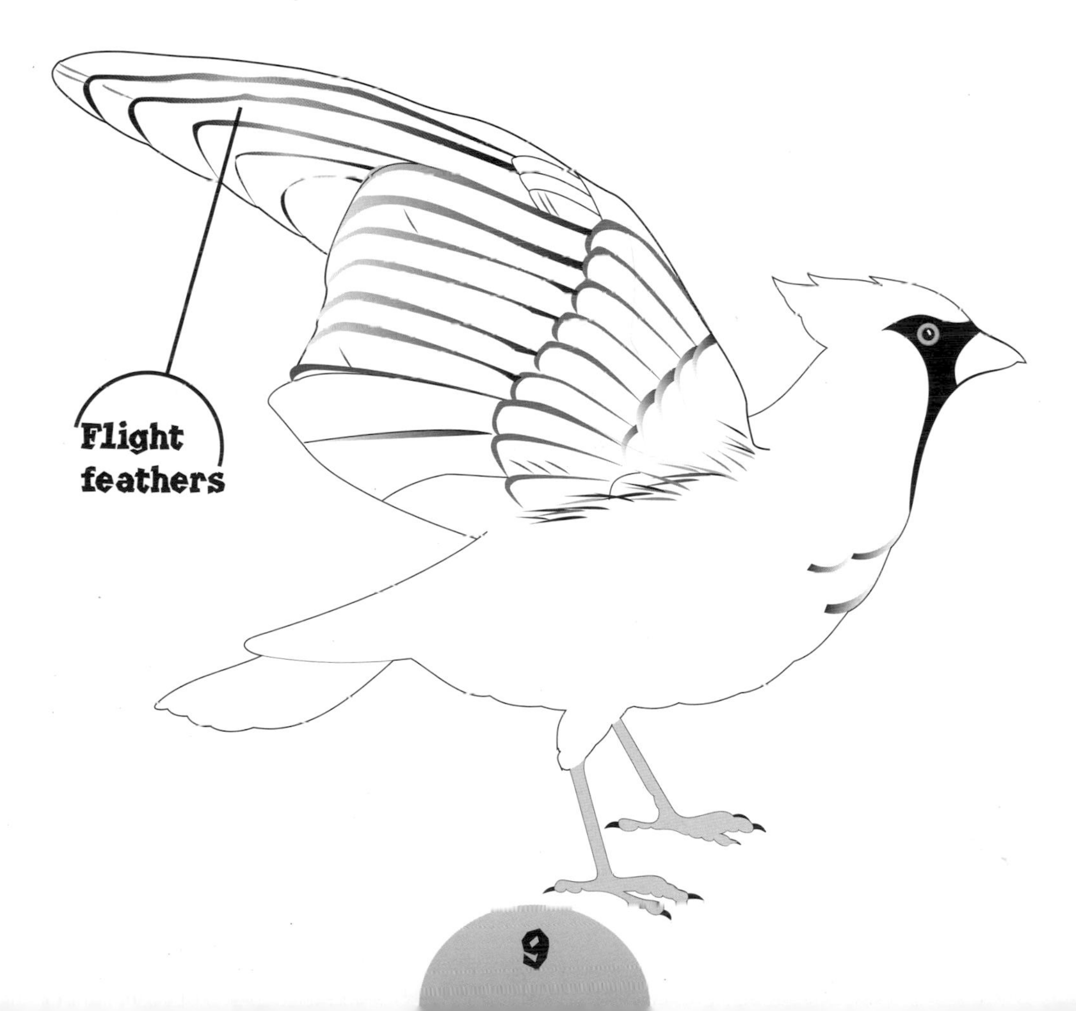

# Where They Live

Cardinals are common throughout the United States. From Arizona to Minnesota, you can find cardinals. Cardinals choose to live in places with bushes, trees, and shrubs. They live in both **rural** areas and cities.

Geese migrate south for the winter.

Some birds **migrate** south in the winter. Cardinals do not migrate. These birds can live in the cold. Some cardinals live as far north as Canada.

# Nests

Cardinals build their nests in many types of trees and shrubs. They nest in hidden, covered places high off the ground. Cardinals build their nests with sticks, twigs, weeds, and leaves. The female cardinal commonly does most of the nest-building work. Building a nest may take many days.

A bird's nest

# Eating

Cardinals eat many kinds of food. These birds have a thick, cone-shaped beak to crack open seeds. Cardinals also enjoy berries, fruits, and insects.

Shrubs with berries may bring cardinals to your backyard.

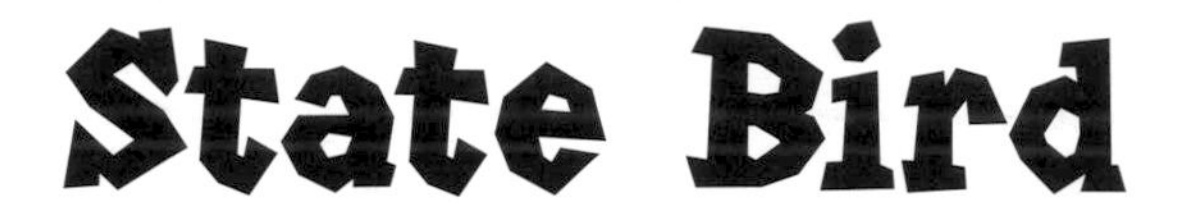


The cardinal is the state bird of seven states in the U.S.

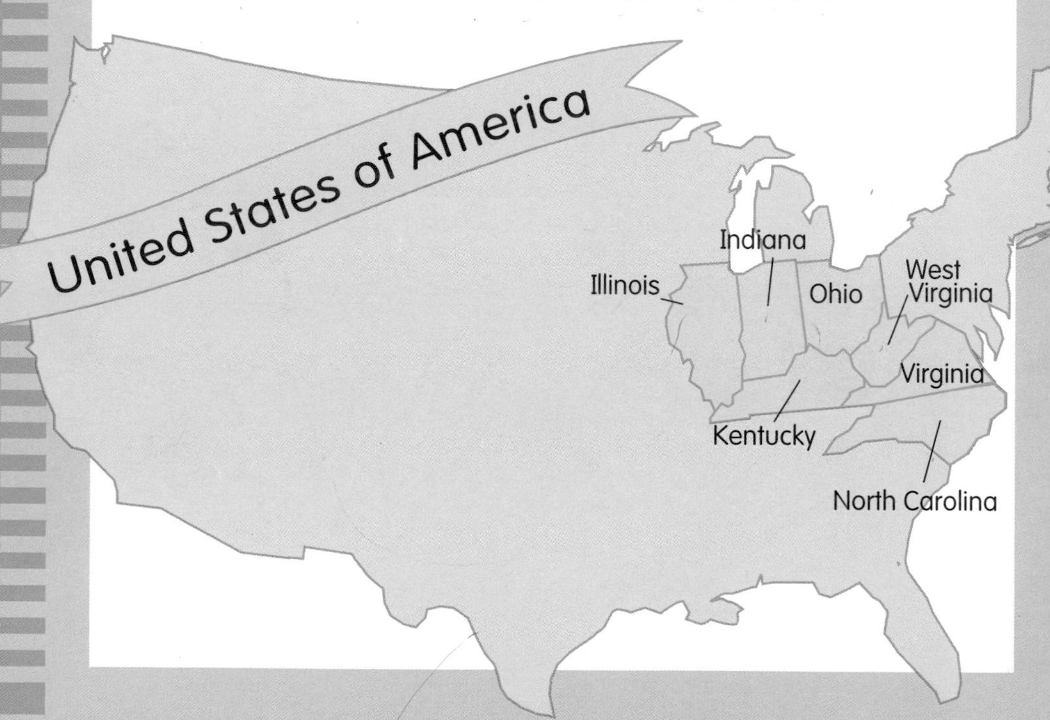

# Cardinal Chicks

Female cardinals lay three or four eggs at one time. Cardinal eggs are grayish white or greenish white. Cardinal eggs have brown spots, too.

The mother cardinal keeps her eggs warm by sitting on them. This is called **incubation**. Incubation lasts 12 or 13 days. After hatching, cardinal chicks are helpless. Cardinal parents keep their chicks safe and warm. They feed their chicks insects. In three or four weeks, these young cardinals begin flying.

A cardinal father with his hungry chicks.

# Backyard Cardinals

Many people like to feed the cardinals living in their backyards. These backyard birds will eat from hanging feeders or off the ground. You can feed cardinals millet, safflower seeds, and cracked corn. Yet, cardinals like black oil sunflower seeds the best.

Cardinals and other backyard birds use birdbaths.

Cardinals also use backyard birdbaths. Birdbaths give cardinals drinking water and a place to bathe. A heated birdbath will not allow the water to freeze in the winter.

# Important Words

**crest** the feathers standing up on a cardinal's head.

**incubation** keeping eggs warm before they hatch.

**migrate** to move from one place to another when the seasons change.

**rural** open land away from towns and cities.

**species** living things that are very much alike.

# Web Sites

## All about Birds

www.enchantedlearning.com/subject/birds/
Learn about bird watching, early birds, and bird fossils.

## Northern Cardinal

www.mbr-pwrc.usgs.gov/id/framlst/i5930id.html
Hear the cardinal's song at this fact-filled web site.

## National Bird Feeding Society

www.birdfeeding.org
This site features a special project for kids that teaches about backyard birds.

# Index